Tripping the Light Ekphrastic

Tripping the Light Ekphrastic
and Other Inspirations

by

Ronnie Hess

© 2022 Ronnie Hess. All rights reserved.
This material may not be reproduced in any form, published,
reprinted, recorded, performed, broadcast,
rewritten or redistributed without
the explicit permission of Ronnie Hess.
All such actions are strictly prohibited by law.

Cover design by Shay Culligan
Cover photo *Afro-Cuban Dancer* by Edie Swift. Reprinted with
permission of the photographer.
Author photo by Martha Jackson Kaplan

ISBN: 978-1-63980-206-7

Kelsay Books
502 South 1040 East, A-119
American Fork, Utah 84003
Kelsaybooks.com

Acknowledgments

The following poems, some in slightly different versions, have been published in these literary publications and endeavors, in print or digital format.

Allegro & Adagio: Dance Poems: "The Dance Competition"
Arbor Vitae: "Art Lesson"
Ariel Anthology: "Ode to a Barred Owl"
ArtAsPoetryAsArt 2019–2022: A Collaboration of Poets and Artists, coordinated by the Lakeshore Artists Guild, Manitowoc, WI: "On the Way to Dock Tarn," "This Time of Year"
Bramble: "Innocent Words," "Standing Before the Ruins of a White Birch," "A Mother's Vinaigrette in Bruges"
Ekphrastic Review: "Genyornis Newtoni," "On Seeing Augustus John's Portrait of Marchesa Casati," "The Chess Game," "Starry Night Over the Rhone," "The Bad Waiter," "On Seeing Marianne von Werefkin's Windblown," "On Seeing Piet Mondrian's Composition with Blue"
Hummingbird: "Medusa Lives"
Madison Museum of Contemporary Art: "Conversations on Seeing Kandinsky's Mural," "Whose Blue?"
Moss Piglet: "One-dimensional Photo of an Aging Couple"
Persimmon Tree: "The Secret"
Poetry Hall: "Ode to a Roach"

Wisconsin Fellowship of Poets (*Museletter* and *Poet's Calendar*): "At the Cloisters Museum," "Visiting Loxahatchee," "On the Métro to Melun"

To the members of my poetry group who made so many of these poems possible—Alice D'Alessio, Martha Jackson Kaplan, Jackie Langetieg, Kathy Miner, Mary Rowin, and Sandy Stark; and in memory of Roberta Krinsky.

Contents

Art Lesson	15
Starry Night Over the Rhone	16
The Bad Waiter	17
Conversations on Seeing Kandinsky's Mural	18
On Seeing Marianne von Werefkin's "Windblown" (1910)	19
Whose Blue?	20
The Martyrdom (1984)	22
Standing Before the Ruins of a White Birch	23
After Shakespeare's Sonnet 141	24
Visiting Loxahatchee	25
On Drought During a Time of COVID	26
The Local Photographer	27
企鹅 Qì'é/Penguin	28
The Secret	29
Genyornis Newtoni	31
Child with Large Bird	32
Ode to a Barred Owl	33
Ode to a Roach	34
Medusa Lives	35
On the Métro to Melun	36
On Seeing Augustus John's Portrait of Marchesa Casati (1919)	37
The Chess Game, 1555	38
On the Road to Dock Tarn	39
Letter Sent, No Address—Dear Frauke	40
Innocent Words	41
On Contemplating a Vincent Van Gogh Landscape at the Metropolitan Museum	42
At The Cloisters Museum	43
A Mother's Vinaigrette in Bruges	44

Reflections on George Ault's Painting "Hudson Street" (1932)	45
Blue and Green	46
Branches	47
Amblyopia	48
One-dimensional Photo of an Aging Couple	49
This Time of Year	50
Foolish Alice	51
On Seeing Piet Mondrian's Composition with Blue (1937)	52
The Dance Competition	53
A Portrait of Flight	54

"Art offers two great gifts of emotion—the emotion of recognition and the emotion of escape. Both take us out of the boundaries of self."
—Duncan Phillips, Phillips Collection

"Come, and trip it as ye go, /On the light fantastick toe."
—John Milton, "L'Allegro" (1645)

Art Lesson

—after Stephen Dunn

A museum guide once held my underarm
and my sister's, ostensibly
to point out light and lace,
the details of 17th century Dutch paintings.
C'est fou, he repeated several times.
She and I were young and nubile.
He pressed his fingers into our flesh,
pulled us around the exhibition rooms.
We were too shy or good
to think the worst,
to free ourselves, and
painting's loveliness
kept us in thrall. We nodded,
learned. Art is not
what you expect, brings you
to the cutting edge of the canvas,
leaves wounds.

Starry Night Over the Rhone

—after the painting by Vincent Van Gogh (1888)

      To have seen it his way,
celestial fireworks, the heavens
revealing the universe beyond his brushes,
the histories of it, its most intricate corners,
dark holes, fierce explosions, disappearances.

      To be dazzled, showered in rapture.
Even the watery elements turned to stardust.

      We had just gone for a stroll that night,
after checking in to the hotel, resting briefly
before setting off again to find a restaurant
recommended by the owner of the inn.

      We had stood for a long time in front
of one of Lyon's many murals, marveling
at the city's famous residents, their lifelike faces
drawn across the wall. We wandered farther
and came upon the river, the full moon
reflected in it, gently waffled by the waves.

      There were bright lights along the quays,
and voices coming from the bars and bistros,
irrepressible laughter, sounds of contentment
even jubilation, glasses clinking,
echoes of childhood.

The Bad Waiter

—after the painting by Vincent van Gogh, *La Guinguette* (1886)

The bad waiter puts his fingers around the rim of the water
glass, sneezes without handkerchief, asks for your order
two minutes after you sit down. He brings the main course
before you're finished with the hors-d'oeuvres, forces you
to lift your plate to make room, asks how the food is tasting
while your mouth is full, stacks dirty plates in front of you,
perfunctorily hands you the bill. You say he hasn't been trained,
doesn't view the job as a career, a *métier,* unlike the starched
and pressed servers in Paris, who are not snooty or servile
but efficient, pacing the meal, elegant as dancers, stretching,
gliding, holding aloft trays of wine and beer, platters of *coq au vin,
gigot d'agneau,* cheeseboards, lemon tarts, landing these safely,
leaving you to savor the faint sounds of a small orchestra, whispers
of rumor, the beginnings of late-afternoon breezes.

Conversations on Seeing Kandinsky's Mural

A circle pierced
by a dart, a triangle,
a beak, a blue piece of pie.
Playthings, paintbrushes,
colored pencils, white checkerboards,
someone's big foot,
five toenails painted red.
Three women come and go,
follow the museum guard's orders
to stay within the visible frame.
   Who could live in this space,
    among these intersecting lines?
Every object becomes
something else,
starburst or flowerpot,
the underside of a bird,
a green fence.
   I could if I had a huge house
   like Marietta's. The black
   is the more effective ground.
You can see whatever you want,
barbed wire, the boat, the oar,
a horse, a ballerina,
the otter, the dove of peace,
nothing really, nothing,
this fractured, terrified world.

On Seeing Marianne von Werefkin's "Windblown" (1910)

To be able to draw
the blue curve at the hip,
the strength of the arm
holding the washing,
the tension of the sheets
in the wind, the whip
of the line. The women
are taking in the laundry,
struggling before the incipient storm,
rain falling on purple hills,
the pitchfork tree.
Such a distance to cover
across the wide grass,
the red barn so far away.

When you shot yourself
in your right hand
was it really an accident?
You could paint
with four fingers better
than any man.
One appropriated your ideas,
another flaunted his women.
Why were you faithful?
What good did it do you?
In an exhibit devoted
to Kandinsky, you are given
such a small room.

Whose Blue?

> *Everything to me is a jumble of shapes and colors. I want to make something that reminds you of this, but you don't know where it comes from.*
> —Ellsworth Kelly

Ellsworth Kelly's color swipes:
shark fin, mainsail, axe, blade or fan.
The eye wants definition,
the mind chooses words.
Instructions:
turn the painting, your head
this way, that. Think of
my father's last words:
blue is such a lovely color,
his body tucked into sheets swimming with red and green fishes,
his hands running over them.
Think of
a job interview:
What is your favorite color?
Indigo, sunsets in Guatemala City,
hotel walls dabbed
with mosquitoes' dried blood. Of
Colette's short story about Madame Angelier,
vaguely unhappy, going about the town
searching for a blue-glass bracelet, recollected forms,
childhood wonders beyond dreams. Of
an Yves Klein postcard, how he and his friends
divided the world. The friends chose earth
and words, Klein ethereal space,
a monochrome exploration,
blue balloons, blue women, blue universe. Of
Miss Paley, high-school geometry teacher,
chop of steel-blue hair, gray New York City light
outside her window. See how
she draws shapes
on a slate board, explains SOHCAHTOA.

Indian princess, fleet rider in fringed buckskin.
Doesn't it mean everything to you?

The Martyrdom (1984)

—inspired by artist Frances Myers

She stands front and center wearing her true colors:
a heart of love, a dove whose wings fan out across
her breast, and stars upon a skirt tight around the pelvis,
as if she is tied into a corset or a flag. Bound, too,
her long, capable arms. See, her manacled left wrist,
the drops of blood below the barbed-wire neck.
She is so tired, listless. Her head is tilted to one side
as if for all its weight she cannot hold it up. You cannot
see below her cut off legs, her toes, if they are planted,
digging tunnels in the loamy ground. Behind her what
remains are opposing columns, one squared, one round.
Wonder Woman, Mother of Peace, Lady Liberty.
Does she dare imagine the silvery bracelets, their youthful
brilliance, the ringing music around the marbled halls?

Standing Before the Ruins of a White Birch

A tree that grew beyond its means, three massive wings
on a trunk that couldn't bear the height, cracked in a storm.
And so it all comes down, branch by branch this morning,
the leaves rustling as they are thrown, the woodcutter
high in his red metal cage, footed like a giant insect on the lawn.
I stand and watch the work, the shredder's teeth being fed
by another laborer's bare hands. It is not my house beneath
the birch and yet I claim it as I do the others along my street
that are not surviving—the plum tree with its memories
of purple studded cakes and jams, the thinning
arbor vitae. Summer edges now to its usual close.
A friend says she has celebrated too many birthdays,
long enough, just let them go, no candles, singing.
The winds pick up, darker, cool these short evenings.

After Shakespeare's Sonnet 141

—In faith I do not love thee with mine eyes

In faith—I would scarcely call it that.
I'd have to be much younger, taut
as a drum, and wattle-free to catch your eye.
But still, I love you with my body. You ignite
my sensibilities when I spy you on the street,
or on a TV screen. Who says desire leaves us,
as do our children, as if the heart dies and with it
all its willfulness: Longings, sighs, laughter,
contentedness. You've heard the story, the crone
in the old folks' home, rumors of her lustiness
as she wanders down the halls, opening doors not her own,
or blowing kisses in the dining room, winking.
Inside my youthful soul there's a smoldering fire.
In dreams, I hear the curly-headed boy playing his lyre.

Visiting Loxahatchee

—after a painting by Kerry Eriksen

Children come to spot the alligator,
run around the pool in front of the nature center,
and out toward the Everglades, whooping and growling,
showing off their youthful fearlessness. But we were here
for silence in the face of expectation, the knowledge
that our world would become splintered sometime soon.
The 'gator slid through the waterways, almost unseen.
Our parents were getting old. They took us to Loxahatchee
the way foreigners show tourists the sights. Northerners,
they were fascinated especially by the birds—the anhinga
perched on a skeleton tree, spreading its wet wings,
dangerously, in the sun; the coots strutting
in the muddy bottom lands; and great blue herons,
dancers on tender legs, spearing prey with their bills.
One late afternoon, buzzards gathered
near the viewing platform and a hot wind thrust itself
in our chests, a warning to measure the land,
our delicate place, the painful balance in wildness.

On Drought During a Time of COVID

Our best work derives merely from a continuity of our daily selves.
—William Stafford

The poets at the virtual conference said, go live your life.
Clothes need folding, dinner cooking, floors to be swept.
Watch the birds, take a walk. Write when you have something.
Last night, we watched The National Theatre's production
of *Romeo and Juliet.* Couldn't stay with it, couldn't
bear the collective suffering. Turning off the TV, we wrote
our own ending, the potions were well-timed, the couple awoke
at the anticipated moment, hugged, became exiles, lived
in another city, had babies, many of them, who did not succumb
to illness, die young, who played well together around the house.
Romeo got a job he liked; Juliet's poems were published.
Among her books: *Love Suddenly, First Light, Fleeting Present.*

The Local Photographer

Each Fourth of July she photographs the neighborhood
celebration: the four-block parade, the rag-tag band,
children on done-up tricycles (red-white-blue), the games:
cakewalk, box-maze, face-painting, egg toss. And the smoky
brat tent, plastic-gloved hands serving food to the crowd.
It is only weeks later that she posts the photos, and I am reminded
as I always am of the luck-of-the-draw, being born into a place
of rare trouble—the occasional car theft, garbage cans not taken in.
Each child's face is like a painting, whether pensive or joyous,
timid or assured, children of privilege, comfort, good schools,
dental plans. There are no cracks yet in the canvas, no suggestions
of what awaits them, flood, drought, devastation. How happy
they are this moment, still under our protection, assured nothing
untoward will happen. The Republic, a piece of earth, still stands.

企鹅 Qì'é/Penguin

      Qì'é—chee-uh,
she says, and it is difficult to get
the correct intonation, the nasality of a final syllable.

      Qì'é—chee-uh.
The word sounds like something vocalized by a bird,
an insect or a frog, deep-throated from a pond.

      Qì'é—chee-uh.
It means penguin in Chinese, her favorite animal.
But here in this other country, even with Chinese adoptive
parents, English is taking over the contours of her mouth,
her body, growing quickly now beyond its orphan size.

Her mother and father speak to her in English with the calm
authority and affection of parents. How easy it seems it has been
for them, how natural, much like the robin in the nest built
on a step of an outside staircase, not a tidy nest, the edges of twigs
and casings extend crudely beyond the cup, still functional.
She sits there day after day through Mother's Day, Father's Day,
intuitive, patient, minding a calling deep in the flesh.

It isn't chicks we should be drawn to but parents,
living beyond boredom, finding food, programmed to duty,
an aching effort, a sacrifice.

The Secret

she was two
she sat on my lap
her small arms
across mine
her words soft winds
or fish bubbles in a stream
how brilliantly she spoke English
given her age
she leaned in
she asked me
if I could keep a secret
my ear tingled
as if it had been kissed
I said of course not knowing
what would come next
the confession of
some night terror
or a prank she had played
a toy broken
a cat's tail pulled
I worried I might
tell someone perhaps
her mother or let it slip
some night exchanging
intimacies with a friend
I considered my own secrets
the ones I tell no one still
after all these years ashamed
but shame did not propel her
our exchange was rather
all about the charm
with which she would draw me in
as a temptress holds out jewels
tresses or her tongue
was her secret about love?

was there one at all?
could I make out the whisper?
that molten confidence?

Genyornis Newtoni

O, biggest of big birds, three times the size of an emu, 500 pounds
of muscle, bone—early hunters may have tracked you too hard

across the Australian landscape, poached your eggs buried
in sand. Or was it the earth went dry, a kind of global warming?

You were the Pleistocene's passenger pigeon, dead as a dodo,
giant Moa, great Auk, Carolina parakeet, elephant bird.

Like a police detective contemplating the body, you ask
what happened or who did this to you, not what medium

was used: Charcoal, clay, shell, amalgam of powders,
not whether the painter was extinction's blind culprit.

Isn't the story in the telling? To see is to be responsible.
Giant ibis, New Caledonian owlet-nightjar, birds in our backyards.

Child with Large Bird

—after the painting by Emil Nolde (1912)

We can only see ourselves as we are.
Our jaundiced shoes, fire-engine socks, hair,

lips, cheeks. Our eyes only have three
color cones. From an evolutionary

point of view, that's enough to make
significant decisions—when to marry,

how to leave, what to wear in disguise.
But birds have eyes capable of

ultraviolet wavelengths. The raven
then is not a black but rainbow-bird

encompassing all hues, beyond blue
iridescence, with a yellow gaze,

recognizing faces from a distance.
Which is the child, which the bird?

Visionary, not omen, sign of war, our own despair.

Ode to a Barred Owl

In the tree above our heads
At breakfast
A hand's length
From the back porch chair
Stately, your round charmed face
Better than fried eggs
Even coffee

Ode to a Roach

The exterminator came the other day.
          He missed you
          or rather in that sprayed
          moment you
          outlived the insecticide.

Late last night you
          peeked up from
          the kitchen baseboard,
          then retreated
          to your New York underworld.

Was that you
          this morning, dead
          on the tiled floor?
          Or in the porcelain sink
          writhing?

How pitifully loathed you are.

Medusa Lives

Perseus told the gods: Forget about it,
leave the Gorgons alone.
                          And so she walks
this morning brushing   her hair over her face
on the way to work.   Or with cascades of curls
running down her back,   waiting on the airport line.
And just the other day on the crosstown bus,
ringlets she pulled back   from her tawny cheeks.
            O! my lovelies,
            let me look at you.

On the Métro to Melun

The sound of swishing
or hissing
or dry grasses in wind
or susurration
or a parent gently telling a child no
or someone mouthing the equivalent of shame,
even a crackling or crisping of parchment
or a distant music under headphones
lost in translation

On Seeing Augustus John's Portrait of
   Marchesa Casati (1919)

Never heard of her until this morning. And the red hair?
A dye job. My friend Sylvia told me, and she ought to know.

Augustus John, aka Lover Boy, cut the painting in half, saved
the private parts, probably for himself. You've got to wonder

why men insist on controlling women, living off muses, sirens,
she-devils with ruby red lips, stiletto heels. What did she ever

do to deserve the honor, or is ignominy a better word? Don't
tell me she held the cards. Without her papa's money, title,

she would have been called a tramp, like the little girls
from the provinces, laboring under a hot sun, out on the streets.

She was an orphan, died poor, buried with a stuffed dog
and her fake eyelashes. So much for mythology.

The Chess Game, 1555

—inspired by Sofonisba Anguissola

The season I was seven and rambunctious,
Paul Cornyetz taught me how to play chess.
He took the chessmen out of a pine box,
placed them on the checkerboard on their appointed squares,
explained to me what moves each piece required,
and why.

I was alone that summer, my mother and sister
away at dance practice, my father working in the city.
Paul and his wife Bernice were taking care of me.
I can't remember a single thing we did together,
just the chess game, Paul's long, perfect fingers,
his intent appreciation. He wrote instructions for me,
his penmanship precise, achingly fine.

I sensed chess required diligence, anticipation,
the memory of moves played and moves imagined.
Something mathematical, formulaic. It was a man's
game, strategic, and I would not be tamed.

There was nothing I could see about romance and passion,
fashionable Italian silks, sisters—their hair done up in braids –
competing. Nothing about the exciting power of knights, bishops,
a Queen, the prospect of toppling the King.

On the Road to Dock Tarn

—after Judith LaGrow's painting *Step into the Woods*

There are many visions along any path,
past the village, along Willygrass Gill,
      up and down
      the ladder stiles,
      towards Lingy End,

           through the woods
           climbing
           the stone staircase.

Once over the hill,
rock gives way to heather, bracken, bog,
the lake in the distance clear as sky.

The sheep are hefted in these parts, meaning
their sense of belonging has been passed
from ewe to lamb. And in a sense, so are we
hefted, returning year after year. Standing here,

      in late September, you might marvel
      over whose hands stacked
      the stones, one by one,
           whose work underfoot
           surpasses us.

Letter Sent, No Address—Dear Frauke

I didn't understand the irony of your name that day,
little lady from Fulda, Germany, you so tall in lime-green
parka, the wind slicing across the hillsides, signs of rain.
It was the time of the new moon and a bard on a rock
was sketching pictures not of the old stone circle but
the people brought there by its history, mystery, Neolithic
charm, plus the sheep were fun for the children to chase.
Strangers cross paths all the time in the English Lake District.
Why should they speak, ask you to help them with quandaries?
Yet you did. You were indecisive about swimming the race.
We were just a couple with our share of issues.
I hope your foot is healed now and you are in the pool again.

Innocent Words

—after the New York Times article by Gal Beckerman*

From 30 boxes, 200,000 documents
powdered with dust, chewed on by mice,
unpacked now—artifacts, unseen
poems, songs, even jokes from ghettos
and camps, neatly compiled on scores
of notecards, in miniscule cursive,
including words like:
Abgang (exit) and *Evakuierung* (evacuation),
innocuous, "innocent," euphemisms
for deportation and death,
ephemera exposed.

One of the last great remaining archives of the Holocaust.

Philologist Nachman Blumental,
a man in owlish glasses,
published one volume of his dictionary,
the letters A through I,
a linguistic grid of Nazism,
extra-personal and personal,
about, too, his wife and son Ariel,
their executions researched, noted
phrase by phrase, a piece of the child's
small leather shoe, retrieved.

Words and their usage as the clearest window into human culture.

Locksmith, if he could have completed a key
for the postwar trials, explained the evidence,
the genocide, reverse-engineered
the German language, history.

* Gal Beckerman, "The Holocaust Survivor Who Deciphered Nazi Doublespeak," *NY Times,* June 24, 2019.

On Contemplating a Vincent Van Gogh Landscape at the Metropolitan Museum

Same approach only different.
Emphasis on the horizontal
but not without a sense of movement,
      the wind blowing the grain, sunflowers,
          this line,
               then another,
                      and another,
building through fields trees hills.
    The cypress, that interjected green
like a church spire.
      Holy. Energy earth and sky. Roots rooted, flying.

Move higher. Let the wind
    release its breath.
Yellow my hands my hair.
    These red dots here.
And here. Like Seurat. How did he do it?

Meaning?

At The Cloisters Museum

the old tapestries are hung in dim light
to hold fast the colors, the rainbows
of threads painting a thousand kinds
of flowers. And in the grass a scattering
of bunnies and birds. The square-jawed men
with hunting dogs and lances have set out
to kill (or at best corral) the unicorn,
to run their metal through its flank.
Strange how grandmothers bring children
into these rooms, where cruelty is rendered
beautiful, yet terrorizes the infant heart.

A Mother's Vinaigrette in Bruges

I wonder, have I birthed an anguished child?
In this sacred city, can I show her joy?
Martyred saints bleed on museum walls.
She suffers through the lanced torsos,
the satanic worlds. In the restaurant one night,
eating sole, boiled potatoes, salad, I offer her
a passport to distraction, an art lesson, perhaps.
I take a stainless-steel soup spoon, the large
European kind, place salt, pepper, three parts
oil and one of red-wine vinegar into the bowl.
I stir the ingredients with a fork.
It is the least bitterness of the day.

Reflections on George Ault's Painting "Hudson Street" (1932)

Dare to smooth over it,
iron out life's complications—

these earthy reds, this structural simplicity,
familiar buildings, neatly lined up,

streamlined, synchronous, alliterative,
floor by floor, windows dark and blank,

brownstones without drama,
water towers dripping no leaks,

smokestacks belching no smoke,
streets without people,

the gritty landscape of the exterior cleansed,
leaving only what you would make of it.

There is no confused child, head in curls.
There is no blood on the sidewalk.

Here, no police, nobody jumped.
Mrs. Figueroa wasn't stabbed to death

in her fourth-story apartment
by the distraught man she had refused.

She was so near to God, top floor,
the sky's three perfect clouds.

Blue and Green

—inspired by a painting by Georgia O'Keefe

The summer I was twenty-one,
friends and I circled the Peloponnesus.
The heat was intense, the land denuded,
Greece's fertile gardens reduced over centuries
to olive and scrub. We toured the sites—
Olympia, Delphi, the oracle.
I did not drink from the stream.
But it wasn't ruins or the talk
about wealthy nations stealing provenance
that drew me. It was the Gulf of Corinth.
With each wave of my hand through water
it turned from dark blue to aquamarine.
I, so used to sea green, to sand instead of rock.
The next morning we breakfasted
on the hotel's stone veranda.
The day was scarcely up. Honey and butter
pooled together as the sun reached my plate.

Branches

> —inspired by a painting by Ignasi Mallol (1922)

Art is an exercise in perspective, drawing objects
on a two-dimensional ground, as if to illustrate
height   weight   heft

Adobe house, up from silty anchors before turning
right to follow the sky.

Trees know which way to turn, up from soil,
headed west   headed east
leafless this time of year,
skeletal,
yet in conversation with framing plane trees
or perhaps olives,
sentinels to the left
and around the town.
Two sailboats moored,
center sand.

Poetry is an exercise in perspective, drawing objects
on a two-dimensional ground, as if to illustrate
time passing   time recovered,
rumors of war, loss,
organizing coin of another realm.

This line across this page, turning,
            an indentation,

a stanza break,
stabs at irregularity

Amblyopia

Right eye early on dominant learns to take up
the load for the weaker one, congenitally defective,
loose-limbed, unresponsive to patches, exercise,
although surgery helps. Still, there's no going back.
Not exactly Cyclops but each eye on its own:
Squinty left far-sighted to the other's nearsightedness
offering least balance to off-kilter sight.
Upshot, without glasses, two of everything,
auras, halos, ceiling lights, double-minded messages
to the brain to live with ambiguity, flux.
Hens are two-eyed but differently—sentinels and sleepers,
one orb programmed to watch while another dreams.

One-dimensional Photo of an Aging Couple

What I look for is family resemblance, generations of DNA exchange. She's my great-great-grandmother Fredericke, born probably around 1820.

She would have been in her dotage here, along with her husband Aron, parents to ten children and perhaps others who did not make the genealogy charts.

She's got my aunt's sneer, a jaded way of looking at things, as if she's been interrupted from something more important, but she's doing it for him, or the ages,

holding his left hand with hers. He's the only one whose genes I hope to mirror. He's calm, almost demure, his right arm at her elbow, wearing a long, dark

woolen coat. It's perhaps October and he knows winter's coming. The apartment or the artist's studio may be cold.

I want to tell him everything's fine now, although time has not been kind. Their youngest son Herman broke from the brood of brothers and sisters, sailed

across an ocean to Sweden, married a woman not his kind, whose children weren't ashes from the fires of World War II.
A surprise to have been mailed this photo in my own old age

by a woman a little younger. Says she's related. Cecilia from Scandinavia. Her offering, an extraordinary gift.
Why is she piecing together a family history of loss?

This Time of Year

before the hours change
the sun shadows leaves
on my wall,
Japanese brush paintings
with barest of movement,
enough to keep me
in my bed.
Cross-hatching of twigs,
branches trimmed.
At some point the leaves
will release, fall
all at once, rain drops
but bigger, softer,
gentle scraps
of paper, green shower
its own replenishing.
Soil accommodates
a ginkgo's largesse,
mulberries, too,
this deliverance,
a mottled carpet,
box of jewels,
jade carnelian garnet agate,
names that open the earth.

Foolish Alice

—for Peggy Rozga

To drink from a bottle of no return,
eat from a cake with no ingredient list.
Yet, childhood is so much trust and blind
experience. We never stop inquiring.
The body is our being and our undoing.
Our shoes too big, the bed too small,
the nipples one morning hardened,
next, the blood cramping along our legs.

I once sat in a hotel room with windows
in the ceiling, sky the only reference point.

I once feared every teacup from a stranger might contain LSD.

In that fearful dream time,
people fell out of windows,
raced about raving,
dropped down rabbit holes.
The boy I dated, dead now, was eager
for cocaine hallucinations.
Sitting astride an armchair, as if on a toadstool,
I said, *something else,*
meaning let's not talk about this.
Yes, he replied, misunderstanding,
something else.
The shock of his black hair over one eye,
so very straight for the bent world
we traveled through.

On Seeing Piet Mondrian's Composition with Blue (1937)

Surely, as his days
became numbered,
my father looked
through the window,
its interstices,
shadows walking by,
hallucinated, perceived
one square of blue,
an infinite sky.
How else to explain
his last words,
about blue being
such a lovely color.

The Dance Competition

It isn't possible to see her face,
only her jet-black hair shiny like glass
pulled tightly back into a bun.
And her siren-red dress, slit at the thigh,
the pink high heels, her feet on tiptoes
to reach him since he is so tall.
She has put one hand around his neck.
His face, on the other hand,
is turned toward us.
His eyebrows are lowered, eyes closed.
His mouth is tight, as if to silence a cry.
He seems overcome, almost shattered.
Is it pain he's feeling? Or could it be joy?
Have they lost the competition or nailed it?
Either way, it's hard to tell
as he stands there, his long arms around her back,
his feet in black shoes perfectly together.
Either way, it would be hard not to love them, him,
alone with her on the dance floor, spotlighted,
while the judges stand in the darkened hall
still holding their scoring pads.

A Portrait of Flight

—after a photograph by Lynsey Addario

A friend sends me a photo of the cover of the *New York Times,*
dateline, August 13, 2021, Kandahar, where the Taliban have

reached the outskirts of the city and a family is getting out of
harm's way. Five girls and you assume their mother have packed

their most valued possessions: A duffle bag is strung over one
of the girl's shoulders, a large box sits on another's head. But it's

the youngster on the left of the frame that grabs your attention,
her head covered with an aquamarine scarf trailing to the ground.

There's a flower on the right shoulder of her navy-blue dress.
She's looking directly into the camera, and in her arms a scrawny

spotted brown hen, its feet tied together so that it won't fly.
Who knows where they are going or what will they find

when they get there? One thing's sure—the hen is capital,
currency, sustenance, something to get up for in the morning,

to believe in, like a kind of religion where you can honestly
believe in miracles, even peace.

About the Author

Ronnie Hess is a poet, essayist, editor, award-winning journalist, and the author of five poetry chapbooks and two culinary travel guides (on France and Portugal, Ginkgo Press). Born and raised in New York City, she now lives in Madison, WI. She has served on the Boards of the Wisconsin Poet Laureate Commission, the Wisconsin Fellowship of Poets, and The Friends of Lorine Niedecker. For more information, visit www.ronniehess.com.

www.ingramcontent.com/pod-product-compliance
Lightning Source LLC
Chambersburg PA
CBHW030916170426
43193CB00009BA/876